THE CHILDREN'S ENCYCLOPEDIA

EDITED BY
ARTHUR MEE
Editor of The Children's Newspaper

VOLUME FIVE

THE EDUCATIONAL BOOK COMPANY, LIMITED
TALLIS HOUSE, WHITEFRIARS, LONDON, E.C.4

Chief Contributors to
The Children's Encyclopedia

Literary

MARGARET ASHWORTH
T. THORNE BAKER
HAROLD BEGBIE
JANET BEGBIE
ERNEST A. BRYANT
JOHN DERRY
FRANCES EPPS
CLARA GRANT
ARTHUR D. INNES
RONALD C. MACFIE
CHARLES RAY
C. W. SALEEBY
J. ARTHUR THOMSON

Art

FREDERICK ANGER
HARRY EVANS
A. FORESTIER
J. R. MONSELL
GEORGE F. MORRELL
WAL PAGET
S. B. PEARSE
ARTHUR RACKHAM
T. H. ROBINSON
W. B. ROBINSON
CHARLES M. SHELDON
E. F. SKINNER
S. J. TURNER

Printed in Great Britain by
The Amalgamated Press, Ltd., London

CONTENTS OF THIS VOLUME

POEMS, NURSERY RHYMES, AND MUSIC IN THIS VOLUME

This list gives the Authors with the titles of their Poems, and the first line of each Poem or Rhyme

The Children's Encyclopedia

VOLUME FIVE

THE GREATEST ROMAN OF THEM ALL LOOKS OUT ACROSS THE FACE OF KENT

FULL LIST OF THE STORIES TOLD IN THIS VOLUME

QUESTIONS AND ANSWERS IN THE BOOK OF WONDER

THINGS TO MAKE AND DO IN THIS VOLUME

ALPHABETICAL GUIDE TO THE PICTURES IN THIS VOLUME

The Story of the Boundless Universe and All Its Wondrous Worlds

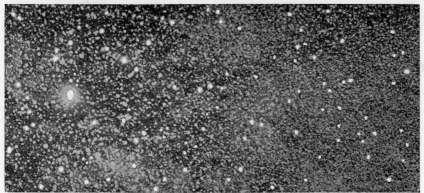

The Milky Way as photographed through a big telescope

THE IMMENSITY OF THE UNIVERSE

WHEN the eye looks upward on a clear night it sees, powdering the dark sky, innumerable points of light which the mind recognises as suns that may be far greater and brighter than the orb which turns our own night into day.

By their double scale, so small to the eye, so vast to the imagination, the stars, as a writer of our own time has said, set before man the double character of his nature and fate. He is himself but a tiny insect on the great Earth on which he lives ; and the Earth is but a pellet in the huge system of the Sun, which in its turn is less than a speck of dust travelling in the immeasurable void of space.

Yet the mind of man is able to grasp these immensities and set them in their proper order. Light comes through the void from the stars to fall on man's eye ; his mind has grasped what that light has to tell him of the distances it has come on its way to the Earth.

The distances are so great that the eye and the mind are the only things by which they can be measured, and if we wish to gain any clear idea of them we can only do so by comparing them with two things that are associated with the human eye and the human mind—the speed of light and the speed of thought.

The speed of thought may have more than one meaning, but here we employ it as signifying the rapidity with which it can transfer itself without pause or interval from the present to the past, or from the Earth on which we live to the farthest planet of the Sun, or to the stars that fringe the Milky Way.

But the speed with which light travels to the eye from the Sun or a star is a more exact thing ; and being, so far as the mind of man has been able to discover, a fixed and unchanging thing, it forms the only gauge by which the dimensions of the universe of stars can be reckoned, and the only unit which gives any clear idea of the size or the shape or the arrangement of that Stellar Universe.

Nearly every one is familiar with some illustration which seeks to show how far the Sun is from the Earth by estimating the time it would take an express train to make the journey. The train which leaves Paddington for Bristol each morning, one of the fastest in the world, would, if it prolonged its journey to the Sun, take some 175 years to get there.

That is, perhaps, not in itself a very helpful statement because 175 years in the future does not convey much to the mind ; but if you can imagine the same train

ASTRONOMY · GEOLOGY · GEOGRAPHY · CHEMISTRY · PHYSICS · LIFE

travelling backward through time, all the events about as far back as the last serious attempt to replace the Stuarts on the throne of England would have time to take place before the journey's end.

THE TIME IT WOULD TAKE A TRAIN TO REACH THE WORLDS IN SPACE

If the train were to make a further excursion, and go on past the Sun to pick up the planet Jupiter on the farther side, its journey would be prolonged for another 900 years. In that nine hundred years everything that has happened since the Norman Conquest could be transacted, all the wars and all the inventions ; and if the train's journey were still farther extended to Saturn (1633 years), or to Uranus (3400 years), it would occupy periods of time which in the world's history comprise not merely the reigns of kings and queens, but the birth and decay of nations.

Finally, before the express reached the outermost planet of which there is positive knowledge, the planet Neptune (5250 years), the journey would have occupied an era in which it would be possible to include nearly all that is written of the civilised world's history, and would easily take in the birth of Abraham and the exodus into Palestine.

These illustrations may convey some idea of the insignificance in size of the Earth when compared with the domain of the Sun and its obedient planets. But they begin to fail when we try to realise the proportion and relation of this Solar System to the star-filled space which the humblest mortal on the Earth can see. Though a hundred million stars reveal themselves in the greater telescopes, the most wonderful, and, indeed, terrifying thing about the space of which they are the tenants is ·its emptiness, and the solitary remoteness of every star from every other.

THE JOURNEY OF 50 MILLION YEARS TO THE SUN'S NEAREST NEIGHBOUR

If that express train which has been used to give an idea of the distances of the Sun and its planets were to be sent on to the star which is the Sun's nearest neighbour, Alpha Centauri, the journey's end would not be reached for fifty million years ; and that figure is merely confusing, because there is nothing in our knowledge of time, even of the geological periods, with which to compare it.

Nor are we much better off if we imagine the distance to be covered by the swiftest projectile ever hurled by the guns of the Great War at a speed, let us say, of 2200 feet a second. Such a projectile would require a million and a half years to reach the nearest star. Even that vast projectile, the Sun itself, which is hurtling through the thinly sown field of stars at a rate of from 11 to 12 miles a second, would, if going that way and the star were standing still, reach it only after some 75,000 years.

Yet there is a measure which can be applied that will bring these distances within reach of comparison. It is the speed at which light travels. Light eats up the miles. It travels a million miles in five and a half seconds. On the wings of light we should reach the Sun in something between eight and nine minutes ; we should be on Uranus before ten thousand seconds had elapsed—which is not very much—and could reach the uttermost limits of the solar system in a few hours.

But if on this magic vehicle we sought the nearest star, the journey through black emptiness would not be finished for four years and four months. The star is twenty-five million million miles away. Consider then how isolated and how small is that solar system which appears so great by the side of the Earth when ranked in the great company of the skies. A rowing boat in the midst of the Earth's greatest ocean is not more utterly alone.

THE INFLUENCES THAT BIND THE SUN AND EARTH ACROSS SPACE

It is only by the exercise of the mind's power of reasoning, and the eye's power of observation, that we can realise that this isolation, which is shared by every other star, each in its own appointed place and solitary state, is only a comparative isolation ; for though there are stars immensely more distant from one another than the Sun and its nearest neighbour, they are bound each to each in some sort of relationship which we know exists, and the secret of which we seek to penetrate. To every star, down to the faintest speck of light that shimmers in the field of the great telescopes, the Sun and the Earth are bound by influences which reach across the void that separates them. Beyond measure may be the influence of these stars, these mighty suns in reality, these specks of bright dust in outward seeming ; but it exists.

We must bear this in mind when we come to consider the further depths of space that the measurement by means of the speed of light enables us, however haltingly, to

THE GREAT GROUPS OF STARS

We give in these pages the groups of stars to which in ancient times people gave the curious names that have become familiar; and our artist has drawn outlines to suggest how their imagination worked in naming these star-groups, or constellations, as we call them, because they appear to cluster together.

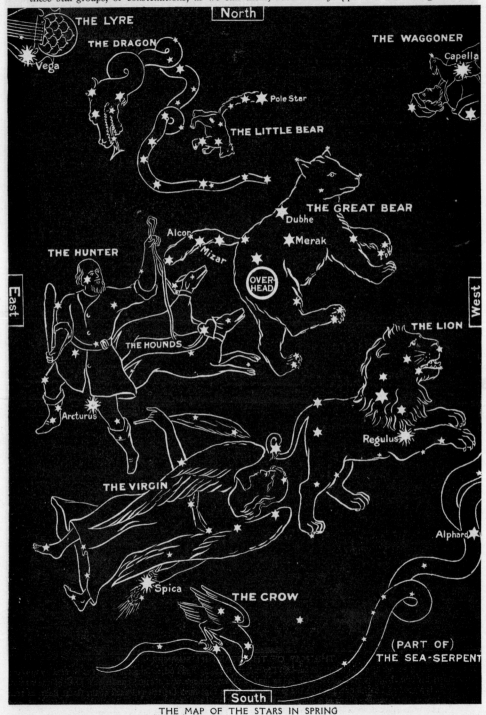

THE LYRE — North — THE WAGGONER — Vega — THE DRAGON — Capella — Pole Star — THE LITTLE BEAR — THE GREAT BEAR — Dubhe — Alcor — Merak — THE HUNTER — Mizar — OVER-HEAD — East — West — THE HOUNDS — THE LION — Arcturus — THE VIRGIN — Regulus — Spica — Alphard — THE CROW — (PART OF) THE SEA-SERPENT — South

THE MAP OF THE STARS IN SPRING

It is often impossible for us to see any resemblance in these star-groups to the creatures after which they are named; but it is suggested that perhaps the positions of many stars have changed, so that we do not see them as the ancients did.

THE MAP OF THE STARS IN SUMMER

The grouping of the stars into constellations supposed to represent animals and other things has been continued by modern astronomers because it has proved convenient for so long, and any change would cause confusion. One of the names, the Plough, is a good and useful one, because the seven bright stars that form the tail and back of the Great Bear, as seen in this picture, really have the shape of a plough. The Great Bear is the most easily seen of all the constellations, and two of its stars point almost in a straight line to the Pole Star, which is always to the north of us.

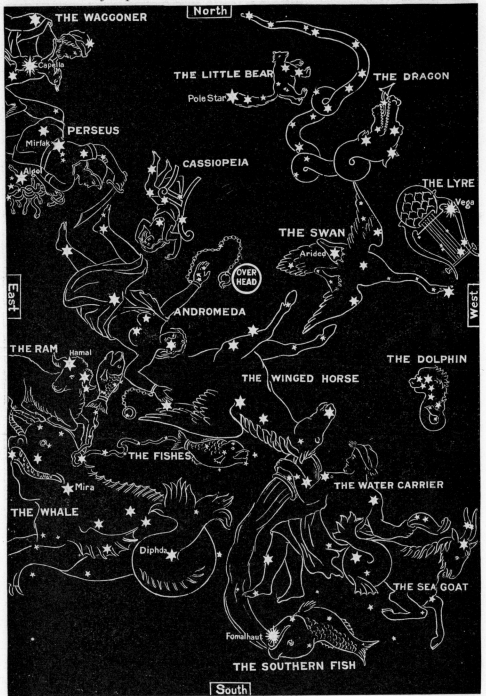

THE MAP OF THE STARS IN AUTUMN

The Zodiac is the belt in the heavens within which the Sun and the principal planets move. The best known of all the constellations are those which lie within the Zodiac. They are twelve in number : the Ram, the Bull, the Heavenly Twins, the Crab, the Lion, the Virgin the Scales, the Scorpion, the Archer, the Goat, the Water Carrier, and the Fishes. We can see all the constellations of the Zodiac in these four star-maps, and can then find them in the sky. These names were given at least 2500 years ago. The Ram and the Archer were the first two constellations to be marked out and named.

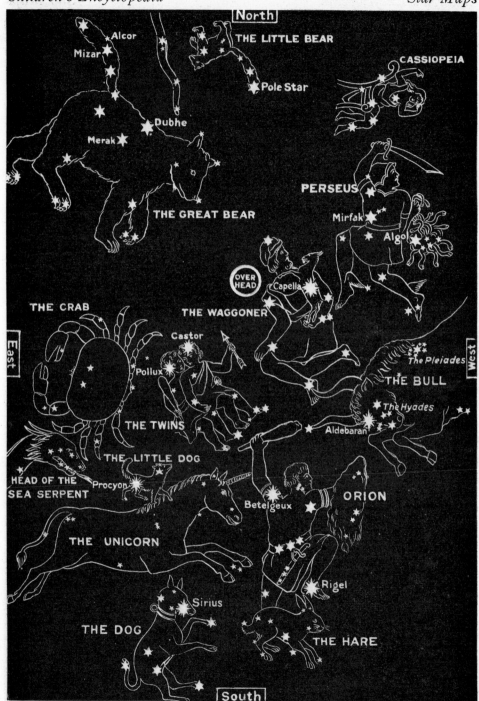

THE MAP OF THE STARS IN WINTER

The two earliest Greek writers whose works have come down to us refer to constellations by the same names we give them. They speak of the Bear or the Wagon, part of which is also known to us as the Plough ; of Orion, whose belt of three bright stars we know so well ; of the Dog of Orion, with its starry nose formed by Sirius : and of the Pleiades. All these are shown here. The Bible also refers to stars and constellations which have been identified as the Pleiades, Orion Arcturus and the twelve signs of the Zodiac. We can read of these by name in the book of Job plumb. So great are their distances, so little perceptible their movements, that of all those bright myriads there are not more than seventy of which we can confidently tell the distance.

The distance of some of the brightest stars in the heavens still eludes us, though, on the other hand, some of them, after years of patient enquiry, have yielded up their secrets. Thus of the brighter stars we have confidence in saying that Sirius, that brightest star of all, is at such a distance that the light it sends to the Earth takes about eight years and nine months to reach us. Altair is 14 years of light-travel away, Aldebaran 30 years away.

Arcturus and Betelgeuse are plunged in a profundity of space so remote from us, that light from them is travelling 126 years before it reaches the Earth. Canopus, the great star of the Nile, bright as it shines, is so far away that the distance cannot be measured. It can only be arrived at by reasoning, which

THE LITTLE DOT WE LIVE ON—EARTH AS A SPECK
IN THE UNIVERSE

takes into account both its brightness and the impossibility of applying any astronomical method of measurement to its never-altering place in the skies.

By such computation it is known that it must be at least 300 light-years away—a

light-year being the distance light travels in a year, at 186,000 miles a second. Consider that distance for a moment, applying it to the methods of illustration that were used when we pictured the railway train travelling backward through time. When the light that falls on your eyes to-night left Canopus, Charles Stuart sat on the throne of England, and the Pilgrims were settling in America.

So far we have been speaking of measures of space which are, by astronomical reckoning, certain and assured. They have been examined by patient and exacting minds for many years, and have stood the test. But it is equally certain that these bright objects of the skies are not the most distant. There are mists and clouds of stars far beyond them, and we know that they must be far more distant because, if for no other reason, they are so less bright.

Canopus is, perhaps, 22,000 times as bright as the Sun. There must be other stars in the firmament as bright or brighter; they do not seem so because they are more distant; and it is on some such assumption as this that their remoteness is estimated. If travelling like light among the stars we scoured the heavens we should encounter, at intervals of years between, systems and suns very unlike our own.

Even that nearest neighbour Alpha Centauri would be very different, for it is in reality two suns. There would be other suns in pairs ; and suns in threes ; and huge suns that could swallow the Sun and its nearer planets with ease ; and great masses of gas like the nebula in Orion, in which the Solar System would be lost.

A WONDERFUL REGION OF HUNDREDS OR THOUSANDS OF SUNS

We should find ourselves in a great region of hundreds or thousands of suns, separated by many years of light-travel each from each, but all travelling in company. This company is called a globular cluster of stars, because it looked, in the older telescopes of last century, like a little fuzzy ball of stars. It was only when the big new telescopes of America and Europe were turned on a cluster like this that it was perceived that the ball contained great numbers of suns, which, like other suns and stars, were of different kinds.

Among these different suns is a particular kind of changeful one, a variable, exactly like a sun near enough for us to estimate its distance. The variable sun in the distant cluster is exactly like the near variable sun in everything but the amount of brightness it sends to us. By estimating this brightness a comparison could be made between its distance and the distance of the variable sun which is near enough to us to have its distance measured. This is the way in which, in the last few years, mainly during the years of the Great War, a new idea was gained of the more immense distances of space.

THE TIME-JOURNEY LONG ENOUGH TO HOLD ALL HUMAN HISTORY

Before that time it was believed that the misty scarf of stars which we see in northern climes on clear nights, called the Milky Way, set the boundaries of the universe of stars. Many estimates had been framed of the distance from which they shone upon us. The best authority, Professor Simon Newcomb, came to the conclusion that the Milky Way in most of its parts was no nearer to us than would correspond to a light-journey of 3200 years. The new inquiries and examination of the clusters of stars put the boundaries farther back than that by far. They put the distances of some of the clusters that are well known and have often been examined at 20,000, or even 45,000 light-years. Some

clusters that are fainter are placed at more than 100,000 light-years ; and the farthest star of all may be as much as 220,000 years of a light-journey away from the Earth.

Even with every aid of the imagination, or with the illustration of the backward moving time-machine of light, that distance is hard indeed to realise, for within that huge gap of years the whole history of mankind could be comprised, beginning with his dim origins in forest and jungle, and continuing with his struggles when, perhaps through some accident in the Sun's own journey through space, he had to battle with the Ice Age.

Even so, speculation as to the vastness of the outermost limits of the universe of stars is not exhausted. Among the wondrous objects in the heavens that the light ray discovers in its journey are the so-called spiral nebulae. No instrument of astronomy, no ingenious computation, has yet certainly made out how distant these are. Some there are who believe them to lie outside the Milky Way and all the ordered regularities of the Stellar System, and picture our universe of stars as speeding forward like a ship through the ocean of space with the globular clusters of stars coming in to join it, and the spiral nebulae speeding away from the prow.

THE TRUTH ITSELF AND THE UNENDING SEARCH FOR TRUTH

It may be so ; these outer systems, if outer systems of stars they be, must yet be joined with the Universe as we see it and know it. Of that Universe we can say with a fine writer, Miss Agnes Clerke, that the scale of its construction strikes imagination impotent ; in the multitudinous splendour of its components, in the number and variety of the groups constituted by them, in the magnificent play of forces it unfolds, it bears glorious witness to the power of the Almighty Designer.

It has its limits, though they be set as far apart as is the east from the west, and for that reason is a fit subject for our limited understanding. Its problems and limits we may never solve completely, but we may remember the words quoted by the astronomer Kapteyn :

If God held in his right hand all truth and in His left nothing but His ever ardent desire for truth, even with the condition that I should err forever, and bade me choose. I would bow down to his left, saying, " O Father give me that, pure truth can be but for Thee alone."

MEN AND WOMEN
The Story of Immortal Folk Whose Work Will Never Die

Sir H. M. Stanley   James A. Grant   Emin Pasha   John H. Speke   Sir R. F. Burton

Sir Samuel Baker   Hugh Clapperton   Mungo Park   James Bruce   Robert Moffat

THE EXPLORERS OF AFRICA

NOTHING more romantic has ever been imagined than the sober history of Africa. The home of Hannibal, of Ptolemy, and of Cleopatra, containing the greatest seat of ancient learning, has remained almost down to the present time the mystery land of the Earth.

Though its northern shores stare across a narrow sea at Europe, and one may march dryshod from Kamchatka to Cape Town, this continent, ancient home of myriads of people, was an unknown land far longer than America.

Hannibal, from his home on the North African coast, dreamed of conquering Europe, but never thought of even knowing Africa. Cleopatra desired no sovereignty over it; the Greeks never penetrated its inner lands; Rome made no serious incursions into it; and the scholars of Egypt knew little or nothing of its dim interior. They only knew the fringe of it washed by the Mediterranean Sea. Their palaces and temples, pyramids and sculptures, dotted its foreshore and lined its one known river, but the rest of the continent might not have existed for all the ancient world cared.

Necho, King of Egypt, as we have read, sent an expedition of Phoenician mariners right round its coast 600 years B.C., and possibly the same adventurous race obtained from some African port the gold for Solomon's temple; but twenty-one centuries passed, and Columbus had more than once crossed the Atlantic, before any voyager repeated the Phoenician voyage round Africa.

It is true the ancients knew of Africa's huge man-like apes, and its tiny ape-like men, the Pygmies, whom no modern man believed in till late in the nineteenth century. Hanno the Carthaginian, voyaging along the western coast, saw, described, and named the gorilla. But when, 2000 years after Hanno, Andrew Battel, a British sailor, who had been a captive for 18 years in Africa, came home and described the African man-beast he had seen he was roundly denounced as untruthful.

Another two hundred years passed, and Du Chaillu actually brought the bodies of gorillas out of Africa, but he, too, was doubted. Yet the gorillas and the Pygmies were there all along, with giraffes, okapis, hippos, and antelopes, peculiar to this great continent. They were first known of there, as was the ostrich, and casual visitors to unfrequented shores, seeing them, and seeing also stalwart man-eating Negroes, were naturally horrified. They fled, warned others of these dangers, and all the world kept away.

All manner of grim exaggerations swelled the terrors of the reality; tales of evil

EXPLORERS · INVENTORS · WRITERS · ARTISTS · SCIENTISTS

spirits, tales of a belt of fire through which it was impossible for human life to pass. Even when Da Gama had sailed round the continent, and it became the practice to visit the African coast on west and east, grave mariners, whose names figure in history, would kneel and pray God that the magic of the savages whose shores they were approaching might not enchant the little ships to their doom beneath the tropical African seas.

There was, of course, a natural barrier parting the north from the interior. The great Sahara desert stretches as a kingdom of desolation south of Morocco and Algeria and west of Tripoli and Egypt. It was a good excuse for those who did not wish to travel south overland, for it was filled with strange fierce beasts and credited with spirits most fell.

THE GOOD EXPLORERS AND THE BAD EXPLORERS OF THE LONG AGO

The early explorers were of two kinds: simple priests who went with incredible daring into realms of benighted savagery to baptise men, women, and children whose very language they did not know; and Spanish and Portuguese slave-dealers who, by the middle of the seventeenth century, were carrying 10,000 poor wretches a year from Africa to Brazil alone, where, toiling like beasts of burthen, the unhappy creatures, if exceedingly strong and equally fortunate, might live out seven years, but not more than seven.

England, to her shame be it told, had her share in those slaves. In the century preceding the American Declaration of Independence, we carried three million African slaves to the New World, and threw another 250,000 into the Atlantic as they died in our ships. All the Negroes in the New World, and they number many millions now, are descended from the slaves stolen with cruelty and violence from the Dark Continent.

Slaves, ivory, gold, diamonds came out of Africa, yet we knew nothing of the interior of the land, nothing even of its shape, nothing of its great rivers. The first real attempt to solve one of the prime mysteries, the mystery of the source of the Nile, was made by a sort of resolute knight errant, James Bruce, a Stirlingshire man, born in 1730, a scholar and business man in whom lived the old Viking strength and courage without the Viking cruelty. His name is for ever associated with Abyssinia.

The Abyssinians believe their kings to be descended from Solomon and the Queen of Sheba. They practised the Jewish religion, and afterward adopted a vague and debased form of Christianity, but when this giant Scot went among them, marching on and on to reach the head waters of the Nile, they behaved in general with treachery and cruelty toward him.

HOW BRUCE OF ABYSSINIA WON HIS WAY WITH THE PEOPLE

But Bruce had a way with him; with his immense courage he had skill and tact. There was help for him in the royal palace, where he cured a royal princess of serious illness and earned her love. Then he passed on and preserved his life by what, to the Abyssinian mind, was wonder-working. He did feats with unbroken horses such as they had never seen, so they gave him a noble horse to drive in front of him, and it proved as sure a passport as was the golden plate which Kublai Khan gave Marco Polo to bring him back to Europe.

The Abyssinians had never seen a gun. Bruce brought down birds and animals with his, and they thought him inspired. They saw him shoot a candle through a stout wooden table with it, and then they were sure he must be a magician. Little by little Bruce gained his object; he reached the source of what he thought was the Nile, but it was only the Blue Nile, the largest of the Nile's tributaries.

His journey was beset with great difficulties and terrible hardships, but in four years he was in and out again, and he returned to Scotland to write a book of the marvels he had seen. It was cordially condemned as romantically but flagrantly dishonest. He went to his grave disbelieved. Later discoveries have entirely confirmed all this strange hero wrote.

THE ADVENTURES OF MUNGO PARK WHO FOUND THE GREAT NIGER RIVER

But if the public made mock of the gallant traveller, here and there brave hearts kindled from his fire. Mungo Park, born in Scotland in the year that Bruce was struggling up-country in Abyssinia, grew up a surgeon, and, thanks to Captain Cook's friend, Sir Joseph Banks, gained experience of strange ways and peoples in far Sumatra, took service with an English organisation called the African Association on the Gambia, learned the native language, and set out to explore the mysterious river Niger.

AS A BOY LIVINGSTONE BEGAN LIFE AT THE LOOM

A savage chief, jealous, like some modern white nations, of a foreigner, imprisoned him ; but he escaped and found the Niger, the great river whose existence had been rumoured but not confirmed, since ancient days. There it was, winding, not westward as tradition said, but to the east. He was not allowed to cross it. " Have you no rivers in your own country, and is not one river like another ? " asked a savage ruler.

ALL THAT WERE LEFT OF FORTY-FIVE GALLANT EXPLORERS

Following the river as far toward its source as he might, Park wandered ragged, solitary, footsore, and ill, but kept all his notes like hoarded diamonds, even when he fell, too weak to walk, and was found by a slave-trader, and carried, almost dying, back to the coast.

He returned to Scotland, married, and settled down, but the call of the East came again, and would not be denied. He returned to explore farther. He got to within 200 miles of that dream of ages, far-famed Timbuctoo, to which the wares of every manufacturing town in England went, but where white men had never been. Disaster dogged his steps. Of 45 companions only seven lived to reach the Niger with him.

From Sansandig he sent back the record of his travels, and they reached England. He never did. His final note in his last despatch valiantly declared, " I set sail to the east with the fixed resolution to discover the termination of the Niger or perish in the attempt." He perished in the attempt.

THE PATHETIC STRUGGLES AND GLORIOUS FAILURES OF THE EARLY DAYS

Through manifold hardships he reached Bussa. There a fatal thing happened. Natives on the spot remembered an earlier Englishman who accompanied native levies as a sightseer on a slave-hunting expedition. They coupled the presence of this new white man with that hated action, and, as he and his four companions were canoeing down a dangerous series of rapids, they attacked them. Whether Park was killed or drowned we do not know, but his splendid life was sacrificed at those fatal falls.

All these early chapters of African exploration are a combination of agonised effort and glorious failure. Timbuctoo and the Niger were names that lured men like magic. Little by little the veil was raised by travellers working south from Tripoli. Men like Ritchie, Lyons, Oundle, Denham, Clapperton, and Lander carried the torch of investigation farther and farther inland, at the heaviest cost a man can pay.

Hugh Clapperton was a great spirit, a Scottish product of the year 1788, who, rising from lowly birth to rank in the navy, went on two great African journeys to the south, and finally reached Lake Chad. He found a city of 60,000 people dealing in English goods and reading classical literature in Arabic translations. He gained the great city of Sokoto, wonderful to us even in our own times ; but he died there in 1827, as his comrades had died before him.

Clapperton had a wonderful servant in the person of Richard Lander, born at Truro in 1805. He was but 20 when his master passed away at Sokoto, but he bore his dead chief's notes back to England, and was himself appointed to carry on the work. He took with him his younger brother John, and these two youngsters renewed the deadly task and traced the Niger to its mouth, proving that it emerges in the Bight of Benin. Yet a third journey the elder Lander made, but this was one too many. He was murdered by natives in 1834.

LITTLE BY LITTLE THE DARK CONTINENT YIELDED UP ITS SECRETS

Little by little Africa was yielding up secrets, some from the north, some from the south, some from each coast. The conquest of Algeria by the French in 1830, and the still earlier passing of Dutch possessions in the south into British hands, made these places safer, as starting points for explorers, and systematic missionary work began among the native peoples.

We must remember that white people and the brown races who invaded the north from Asia are but a minority. The black natives even then numbered scores of millions, and their only experience of white men was that they traded unfairly in native goods, and brutally in human lives.

The first great British missionary to preach a different story was Robert Moffat, of whom we have already read.

Moffat was not an explorer, except of the human heart, but he went crusading into the dreaded wilderness and blazed a trail for searchers of territory. As he wandered up-country from Capetown he

LIVINGSTONE'S LAST JOURNEY

HIS FAITHFUL FOLLOWERS CARRY THEIR SICK LEADER TO THE HUT HE WAS TO DIE IN

Livingstone, falling very ill, begged his faithful followers to build him a hut to die in. " I am very cold," he said; "put more grass on the hut." In the morning they found him kneeling, dead, and carried his body to the ship which was to bear him home for burial in Westminster Abbey.

stopped one night at the farm of an old slave-owning Boer. Asked to conduct a service, he expressed his willingness, but inquired, " Where are your Hottentots ? Are they not to come in ? "

" Umph," said the old man fiercely. " If it is a congregation of that sort you want, I'll call in the baboons from the mountains or the dogs from the porch."

Moffat began his service without another word, but he took for his reading the Bible story in which occur the words, " Truth, Lord, but even the dogs eat the crumbs that fall from the master's table."

The tough old Boer interrupted him, " Will you sit down a minute, you shall have the Hottentots."

THE POOR BOY IN A FACTORY WHO HEARD OF RICHARD MOFFAT

And in they came, wondering. They were seeing the inside of a Christian house for the first time in their lives. When the service was over and the blacks had gone, the farmer said in his rough, kind way, " My friend, you took a hard hammer and you have broken a hard head."

Moffat went up to the wilds of Great Namaqualand, settled at Kuruman in Bechuanaland and transformed that wild and bloodstained land into a sanctuary of Christian light and civilisation. News of his triumphs reached England and stimulated many lofty minds. One of his unknown disciples was a poor boy working in a cotton factory in Scotland, whose name was David Livingstone.

No one ever had a harder struggle to gain knowledge than Livingstone. He wrought early and late, studying his book even when at his labour in the mill. His heart was wholly given to the thought of winning human souls for God.

He longed to do for the people Marco Polo had visited what Moffat was doing for the blacks in Africa, but when he was qualified for mission work, war broke out in China, so he was headed off to Moffat's own theatre, and entered Africa as doctor, missionary, and explorer in 1841, when he was 28 years of age.

A YOUNG MAN'S COURAGE IN THE HEART OF AN APPALLING LAND

With his arrival, exploration entered upon a new phase, a bold departure from south to north. He married a delightful girl Mary Moffat, daughter of his chief, and their married life is a chapter of pathetic romance to be studied for its genuine human interest.

After several years of exciting work in purely missionary effort, Livingstone, repulsed by the Boers in his efforts to found mission stations in the Transvaal, wandered north of Moffat's home, discovered Lake Ngami, and resolved to cross the continent from east to west and from west to east, between the Atlantic and Indian Oceans.

It was a tremendous resolution for a young man suddenly to take in the heart of an appalling land, where all was dark forest gloom and mystery, where every tribe was savage, where animals menaced his life day and night, and fever, pestilence and starvation stalked side by side with him continually. But he did it. In four years he crawled and tore his way from side to side of the Dark Continent, the first white man in the world to do so.

His power over the natives was extraordinary. He went in safety where an army would have been slaughtered. He discovered facts at which the world had never guessed. In that one journey he revealed one of the greatest natural wonders of the world, the mighty Victoria Falls on the Zambesi, which some day will furnish far more power than Niagara does in America.

THE AIM AND END OF ALL THE TRAVELS OF LIVINGSTONE

He came back to England, rested a while, then went back to his work of discovery and civilisation. Wherever he turned he saw the blight of the slave trade saddening the land, and he yearned to master the details of the country so that he might have information for British settlers who should go out to the best places in which to settle, set up honest commerce and so kill the hideous traffic in human beings.

That was the aim and end of all his travels. Those travels are not to be set down in the course of a few lines. He suffered the agony of separation from his beloved wife, when death took her in 1862 ; he endured repeated illnesses from the mischiefs for which a tropical climate is peculiar. But for five years he did magnificent work in discovering Lakes Shirwa and Nyasa and exploring the Zambesi, Shiré and Rovuma, and he actually, with his own hands, navigated a little steamer to Bombay in the track which Da Gama had followed long before.

Returning for a further rest to England in 1864, he was sent back to Africa for the last time in 1865. Reaching Zanzibar in January, 1866, he set out for the interior in the following April. The journey was long and difficult, and he was prostrated by illness and hampered in various ways, basin, which up to that time still remained a blank on the map. He found the river flowing in gigantic volume to the north and thought he had the Nile before him. In this, however, he was mistaken.

SIR SAMUEL BAKER RIDING FOR HIS LIFE FROM A WOUNDED ELEPHANT

SIR SAMUEL BAKER AND HIS WIFE SETTING FREE AFRICAN SLAVES

especially by Arab slave-traders. But after two dangerous years of exploration he discovered Lakes Mweru and Bangweulu and launched out into the mystery of mysteries, the true story of the Congo It was the Congo, but he never knew it. More and more illness and shortage of food and medicines weakened his wasted frame. At last he could go no farther, but stayed, famishing and fever-stricken at Ujiji. There he was found by a man who had been sent out in search of him with food and clothes.

As soon as his health was better; Livingstone went on once more with his work, and never ceased until his last illness came upon him. Then he had to rest at Ilala. He was very ill. " Build me a hut to die in," Livingstone said to his men. " I am very cold ; put more grass on the hut." They built him a hut and left him, and in the morning found him kneeling beside his bed, dead.

The great traveller had been called home to God while he knelt in prayer.

How THEY BROUGHT HOME THE BODY OF DAVID LIVINGSTONE

His loving servants knew that his friends would wish to have him buried in England, so they set out to carry his body all the way to Zanzibar, hundreds of miles away. The savages through whose country they had to pass were afraid of the missionary now that he was dead, and thought that if the body passed that way it would bring evil upon them. So Livingstone's followers made up another package and pretended that the body was in it. This they took back and buried. But the real body they had in a bundle, as if it were merely a parcel of goods, and so got it safely to Zanzibar. From there it was brought to England, and buried in West-minster Abbey, in April 1874.

Before Livingstone died his friends in England had been very anxious about him, not having heard of him for a long time ; and another explorer was sent out to find the missionary. The man who went to find him was Henry Morton Stanley. As a boy Stanley was so poor that he had to go to the workhouse school in the little village in Wales where he was born. His real name was Rowlands, but he went to America when a youth and took the name of Stanley from an American who was a good friend to him. He travelled a great deal, and always did his work so well that the owner of an American newspaper told him to take all the money he needed and go to Africa to find Livingstone.

THE WORKHOUSE BOY WHO WENT OUT TO FIND THE LOST EXPLORER

Stanley did so. He sailed to Zanzibar in January, 1871, marshalled an ex-pedition with abundant supplies, and nine months later came up with the dying man at Ujiji. It was a meeting which will never be forgotten as long as travel records are read.

In his joy Stanley could have wept aloud ; he could have seized this poor stricken hero in his arms and have em-braced him ; but speech faltered on his lips, and he could only bare his head and haltingly murmur the stiff and absurd formality :

" Dr. Livingstone, I presume ? "

Even poor agonised Livingstone could not keep back a smile at this shy hero's absurdity. However, all is well that ends well. The two were at once great friends. Livingstone was fed and brought back to health, and did a great journey with Stanley round the north end of Lake Tanganyika, which they proved to have no connection with the Nile. Then Living-stone wandered away, while the younger man returned to civilisation and fame.

A second time Stanley went to Africa, and after important discoveries in the east, he marched round Tanganyika, and by a brave journey, carried out amid appalling difficulties and dangers, fol-lowed the Congo to where it pours its mighty waters into the Atlantic. He had still further work to do in Africa, for he was sent out in 1886 to rescue Emin Pasha, and succeeded, but at the cost of a disaster to a great part of his expedition, in which many men perished.

THE STRANGE MAN WHO WAS SHUT OFF FROM ALL THE WORLD

Emin was originally Edward Schnitzer, a Jew of Silesia, born in 1840. A doctor by profession, he adopted Turkish manners and religion, went to Egypt and was appointed to high office. General Gordon made him Governor of the Equatorial Province of Africa, and for eleven years this strange and able man remained, a white scholar among sable savages, re-mote from the world, learning languages and customs, geography, meteorology, zoology and botany, where a white man had never lived before. He gave all his knowledge freely to the world, and was esteemed by all but the slave-traders, who found in him a remorseless opponent.

For all those years Emin remained isolated, and at last was completely hemmed in by enemies ; that was why Stanley was sent to relieve him. But Emin's heart was in Africa. He re-turned to his old sphere and was mur-dered by slave raiders in 1892, three years after Stanley had rescued him.

FOUR EXPLORERS OF AFRICA

MUNGO PARK IN PERIL FROM THE MOORS

SPEKE APPEALS TO HOSTILE NATIVES

JAMES BRUCE ON A WILD HORSE TERRIFIES
THE ABYSSINIANS

ROBERT MOFFAT COMES ON THE TRAIL OF
THE SLAVE HUNTERS

These pictures are reproduced by courtesy of Messrs. Seeley Service and A. and C. Black

⁸ B 5

Many other names come into the great story of Africa. We must note two giants in Sir Richard Francis Burton and John Hanning Speke, born adventurers of the best type. Both had had experiences enough to fill many books before the Royal Geographical Society, in 1856, sent them out finally to settle the source of the Nile. Two years of battling with every imaginable difficulty led to their discovery of Lake Tanganyika.

THE PROBLEM THAT HAD PUZZLED ALL MANKIND

They parted for a time on the way home and Speke, when alone, hit upon Lake Victoria Nyanza. Ill-feeling resulted between the two explorers over this turn of fortune, so in 1860 Speke went out again in company with James Augustus Grant, further explored the Victoria Nyanza, and proved it to be a source of the Nile.

A problem which had puzzled all mankind from the time of the Pharaohs was thus settled, but a surprise was to come. Sir Samuel Baker, another Titan of travel, who roamed the world for twenty years before marrying an accomplished and valiant Hungarian lady, set out with her to probe still deeper into the secrets of Africa. They landed as Grant and Speke were returning, and met them to hear the glad tidings that the source of the Nile had been found at last. There was still something to be done, so on went Baker and his lady into the gloomy wilds.

They heard from natives that in addition to the discoveries of Burton, Speke and Grant, there remained to be found yet another inland sea. Baker and his heroic wife were not to be contented till they found it. Find it they did, the Albert Nyanza, as Sir Samuel named it. And here was the joyful surprise; Albert Nyanza is a second reservoir of the Nile.

THE DISCOVERY OF THE SOURCES OF EGYPT'S GREAT RIVER

Bruce had toiled right through Abyssinia only to find a tributary. Expedition after expedition had laid down its life in the hopeless quest of the springs of the river which gives life and prosperity to the land of the Pharaohs, of Cleopatra and the old scholars of Alexandria. Yet now three men and a woman had in five years found the twin sources of the wonderful river, and little children were placed in possession of knowledge which even wise and powerful Moses lacked, and saw a riddle solved which was too great for

Joseph when he translated the dreams of Pharaoh before the Egyptian famine.

Later, Sir Samuel Baker, still accompanied by his devoted wife, did what Livingstone described as a more noble work than the discovery of the Nile sources—he struck the first successful blow for the suppression of the slave trade in the Sudan, in spite of the treacherous evasion by Egyptian officials who were pretending to help him.

The exploration of Africa brings into history a host of worthy names, but we are only looking here at the men who opened its gates, who first crossed the continent, who solved the great mystery of its rivers and great lakes. They were all heroes. They all confronted dangers and horrors unknown in the lands from which they sprang. They faced lions and leopards, hippos and rhinos, lurking jackals and bone-smashing hyenas. They challenged fevers and sicknesses whose seeds even now we are seeking as blind men in unfamiliar surroundings.

THE MYSTERY COUNTRY OF THE EARTH HAS OPENED UP AT LAST

The insects which these pioneers scorned and died for scorning were worse than the ravening lions. A modern poet, studying a great captive lion, has unconsciously written the epitaph of hundreds of men who went out to Africa without hope of profit or renown, simply to extend the bounds of human knowledge.

How came the lion into captivity? our poet asks. A man captured it. And where is that man?

> It was that man who went again, alone,
> Into thy forest dark—Lord, he was brave!
> That man a fly has killed, whose bones are left
> Unburied till an earthquake digs his grave.

That is true of many of the men whose names and deeds march sadly triumphant through the memory of one who ponders the story of the explorers of Africa. The ancients, who thought nothing of preventive medicines against malarial insects, were perhaps wiser than they knew in keeping out of Africa's gloomy heart. They left it for modern men to open up the last mystery land of the Earth, and it has been done.

For thousands of years men dwelt in wealth and luxury on the front doorstep of this continent. We have gone in and possessed it, and those who paid the price would say that the conquest justified the sacrifice men have made.

STORIES

The Great Stories of the World That Will Be Told For Ever

THE MAGIC TINDER-BOX

A HANDSOME young soldier who was returning from the wars with his knapsack on his back came upon an old witch standing in the road.

"Good-morning," she said. "It's a fine thing to be rich, isn't it ?"

"I don't know," returned the soldier. "I've not a penny in my pocket."

The old witch came a little nearer.

"Shall I make you rich ?" said she.

The soldier almost dropped his knapsack in his excitement.

"I wish you would !" he exclaimed.

"Then listen," said the witch. "Do what I tell you, and you shall be. Do you see that tree yonder ? Go near, and you will find a hole in the trunk through which you can let yourself down into a cavern full of treasure. Within are three doors ; open the first, and you will find yourself in a little room. In the middle stands a chest full of copper coins, and on it sits a dog with eyes as big as tea-cups. But have no fear ; pick him up in your arms, put him on this blue-checked apron, and take all you want.

"If you prefer silver open the next door you come to, and you will find another little room. In the middle stands a chest full of silver coins, and on it sits a dog with eyes as big as mill-wheels. But have no fear ; pick him up in your arms, put him on the apron, and take all the silver you want.

"But perhaps you prefer gold ? If so you must go to the third door. Open it, and you will find yourself in another room. In the middle stands a chest full of gold coins, and on it sits a dog with eyes as big as the Round Tower. But have no fear ; pick him up in your arms, put him on the apron, and take all you want."

"I'm sure you're very kind," said the soldier ; "but I'll warrant you'll be expecting a nice little pile for yourself !"

"Not a penny," answered the witch. "All I want is my old tinder-box, which my grandmother forgot to bring up with her the last time she was there."

"Well, that seems a simple enough matter," said the soldier. "But I should like to know how I am to get down ?"

"Fasten this rope round you, and leave that to me," said the witch.

So the soldier climbed up the tree, and the witch let him down through a hole in the trunk. Down, down, down he went, until he landed safely on the floor of a huge cave, which was ablaze with lights.

He found a door, opened it, and there, sure enough, on a chest in the middle of the room sat the dog with eyes as big as tea-cups. The soldier lifted the dog on to the blue-checked apron, opened the box, and filled his pockets with copper coins.

Then he shut the lid, put the dog back on the box, and went out.

IMAGINATION · CHIVALRY · LEGENDS · GOLDEN DEEDS · FAIRY TALES

Just then he caught sight of another door. Turning the handle, he went in. In front of him stood a great chest, and on it sat a dog with eyes as big as mill-wheels, just as the witch had said.

He picked up the dog, set him on the blue-checked apron, and opened the chest, which was filled with silver.

"This is worth having," said the soldier, tossing out the copper coins and re-filling his pockets with silver.

When they would hold no more he replaced the dog on the chest, and was turning to go when his eye fell upon a third door, which he opened. In the middle of the room stood a chest, and on it sat a huge dog with eyes as big as the Round Tower. The soldier was terrified, but, remembering what the witch had told him, he summoned all his courage, lifted the dog, and set him on the blue-checked apron. Then he flung open the lid, and was amazed at the mass of gold coins that lay there.

With both hands he grasped his treasure, and thrust as much money as would go into his pockets. But they were already so full that many of the coins fell out.

"Why should I concern myself with silver when all this gold is mine for the taking?" he thought; and, slipping off his coat, he turned it upside down till all the pockets were empty. Then he re-filled them with gold, shut the box, put back the dog with eyes as big as the Round Tower, and made his way to the foot of the tree-trunk.

"Don't forget my tinder-box," called out the old witch from above.

"That's just what I have done," said the soldier, turning back.

He found the box, and was pulled up through the tree.

"What do you want with this old box?" asked the soldier, as he stood once more beside the witch. "It must be very valuable."

The old woman made no reply, but kept her eyes fixed on the box.

"Tell me the secret of the box—for I am sure there is one—or I will certainly cut off your head," said the soldier.

"Give me my tinder-box!" screamed the old woman. "You have gold enough. Would you rob me of my box?"

"Yes," replied the soldier brutally; and without more ado he drew his sword and cut off her head. Then he picked up his knapsack and went to the nearest town.

There his money brought him many friends. He lived in a grand house and had a number of servants to wait upon him. For a long time, indeed, he lived gaily in great style; but at last there came a day when his money was all spent, and he was forced to move into a tiny room in the poor part of the town.

As he was sitting alone one evening in the dark—for he was too poor to afford a light—he suddenly remembered the old tinder-box. He dragged it from where it lay, almost forgotten, and opened it, and at the bottom, to his delight, he found a few flints. He struck one against the box, but no sooner had the spark appeared than the door of the room flew open, and in burst the dog with eyes as big as tea-cups.

"What commands has my master for his slave?" said he.

The soldier was amazed.

"My word!" thought he. "Then this must be the secret of the tinder-box! It will evidently bring me whatever I want."

"Bring me money," he said aloud, whereupon the creature vanished; but in a few minutes he was back again, holding in his mouth a large bag full of money.

Soon the soldier found out that by striking the flint once the dog that sat on the copper chest came to him; by striking it twice the silver dog appeared, and by striking it three times he could summon the guardian of the gold treasure.

That day there was no happier man in all the town. He returned to his grand house, and once more lived a life of gaiety.

Now, in this town there lived a beautiful princess. It had been foretold that she would one day marry a common soldier, and this so enraged the king that he locked her up in a great copper palace and allowed no one to visit her but himself and the queen.

When the soldier heard this story he determined to see the beautiful princess, come what might. So, summoning the dog with the eyes as big as tea-cups, he bade him bring the princess without delay.

The dog obeyed, and in a short time appeared with her fast asleep on his back. She was so wonderfully beautiful that the soldier bent over and kissed her gently, and then bade the dog take her safely back to the palace.

The next day the princess told the queen that she had had a strange dream. She had dreamed she was riding on a huge dog, and was taken to a soldier, who kissed her.

"A pretty dream indeed!" thought the queen. "I'll find out where she goes."

That night she fastened a little bag of flour to the princess's waist; but before she went away she took out her gold scissors and made tiny holes in the bag, so that if the princess moved the flour would drop out and mark the road along which she travelled.

This is just what did happen. The soldier had fallen in love with the beautiful princess, and that night he again sent the dog to bring her to him; and all the way along, as the dog ran from the palace to the soldier's house, the flour dropped out.

The next morning, when the princess said, "I had that strange dream again last night; I wonder what it can mean," the queen rose quickly, and went to a window from which she could see the roadway. There, sure enough, was the little line of white.

Summoning her servants, she bade them follow that white line and arrest the man to whose house it led; and so, before an hour had passed, the soldier was arrested and cast into prison.

The next day he was to be executed, and as he was sitting in his cell waiting for them to come for him he thought how different things would have been if only he had had time to bring away his tinder-box. Just then his eye fell upon a little shoemaker's apprentice who was passing the window.

"Hi! boy!" he cried, starting up. "Fetch me my tinder-box, and I will give you a gold piece for your trouble."

Away ran the lad in great glee, and was soon back again with the magic box. From that moment the soldier knew his troubles were over. But he allowed the soldiers to lead him to the scaffold; and then, when the king and queen and the whole court were assembled, amid a great crowd of people, to see the execution—just when, in fact, the executioner was on the point of putting the rope round his neck—the soldier turned to the king and said:

"Will it please your majesty that I should smoke one pipe before I die?"

He spoke so courteously that the king consented; and then, in an instant, the soldier drew out the tinder-box. He struck it once, he struck it twice, he struck it three times, and suddenly all three dogs stood before him—the dog with eyes as big as tea-cups, the dog with eyes as big as mill-wheels, the dog with eyes as big as the Round Tower.

"Protect me! Protect me!" cried the soldier. "Don't let them hang me!"

Up sprang the three dogs, and in an instant there was a wild scene such as had never before been witnessed in that city. The dogs dashed in among the people, scattering them far and wide. The dog with the eyes as big as the Round Tower flew at the king and queen, and tossed them high into the air, so that their necks broke as they fell and they were killed.

Then all the people shouted with one voice: "We will have the soldier for our king. Set him on the throne, and put the gold crown upon his head. He shall marry our princess and rule over us."

They flocked to the scaffold and released their hero, while a party of soldiers marched to the copper palace to escort the lovely princess to the heart of the city, where all the people eagerly awaited her. As the procession came in sight they burst out into prolonged cheers, so that it was some time before the Lord High Chamberlain could make his voice heard. And when he announced that the princess had consented to marry the soldier they clapped their hands, and cheered till the streets echoed.

The next day there was a grand wedding. The soldier married the princess, amid scenes of great enthusiasm, and they lived happily together all their lives.

THE KING'S WATCHERS

A CERTAIN king who had an orchard of fig trees prized the fruit so highly that he determined to have the trees guarded. For this purpose he placed in the orchard a blind man and a lame man.

The next day the king found that much of the fine fruit had gone, and he asked the watchers what had become of it.

"I do not know," replied one man.

"Nor I," said his companion.

The king then asked if they had eaten the fruit themselves.

"I could not steal the figs," said the lame man, "for I could not walk up to the trees."

"And I could not take them," said the blind man, "for I cannot see."

But the king was very wise, and he soon discovered that the blind man had carried the lame man, and that while the blind man had used his legs the lame man had used his eyes and hands, and in this way the figs had been stolen. Both the men were severely punished.

HOW RINDAR BROUGHT THE REINDEER HOME

Year after year the ice came farther south. It never melted in the brief, cool summer, and every winter it put forth the terrible fingers that gripped more and more of the land and turned it into a lifeless wilderness.

For many months in the year the Sun was blotted from the sky by fierce and dark snowstorms, and so cold was it that animals froze as they moved about in a vain search for food. First the snow buried them, and then the ice-field moved down and ground them into the earth. Over Ireland and Scotland and the greater part of England reached a vast, unbroken field of ice.

A few huge Polar bears shambled about the ice; the white-haired fox from the North Pole preyed on the flocks of wild birds that came in the brief summer-time to the lands at the edge of the ice. And in the southernmost part of England the great woolly mammoth, with its long, curly tusks, managed somehow to exist on the poor, stunted grasses of the frozen marsh.

Yet amid this white and silent desolation a few scattered bands of human beings continued to live. There were still reindeer in the southern part of England, and still some tribes remained, fighting for a living, on the clear strip of land in England. Chief among them was Rindar, the head of a clan which roamed on the northern bank of the Thames. His territory stretched from the mouth of the great river along the eastern coast as far as Suffolk, where the great ice-field began.

All this really happened a hundred thousand years ago. Yet if Rindar were living at the present time, and dressed in modern clothes, no one would be surprised to see him. He was a tall, strong man, with hair that tumbled about his shoulders. Though he had but rude weapons and tools of chipped stone to work with, his powers of mind were keen. Very different in appearance was he from the savages with low brows and stupid faces who had settled down on the next strip of territory.

Guda, his wife, was a handsome woman for those days, and they had a little daughter, Gud. They were all dressed in thick furs, with a fur hood that almost covered their faces when it was pulled down, and they wore boots made of the fur of animals. For in the height of summer the weather was cold, and in the winter it was impossible to live without the heaviest clothing to protect them.

One winter afternoon Rindar was hunting by himself when a dwarfish savage sprang at him, threw him on the ground, and began furiously to rub his nose in the snow. It was a very friendly action, for the chief's nose had become frost-bitten without his knowing it, and by this rough, prompt action the savage saved the chief from a very bad frost-bite.

That was how the Dwarf, as the fair people called the strange savage, made a friend of the chief. The savage had quarrelled with the head of his own tribe, and was grateful to Rindar for befriending him. His pride at becoming a member of a tribe of fair people consoled him for being an outcast from his own race, and he did all he could to make himself useful to his new friends.

The Dwarf quickly distinguished himself as a home-hunter; he was nearly always the first man to find homes for the tribe.

Rindar and his people could not live in the open air; it was much too cold. On the other hand, they could never stay in one place, for they had to move continually after the herds of reindeer on which they lived. When the tribe moved the Dwarf went in front. Keeping his eyes fixed on the ground, he spied out the footprints of bears, and tracked them to their caves.

There was another thing—and a very daring thing—that the Dwarf did remarkably well. He was the only man who liked to roam about the great ice-field. He would take food with him and be away for days, and he would return with a load of white fox furs, which he gave to Rindar.

But late one evening he came back with an extraordinary gift for Gud, the chief's daughter. He had found a baby Polar bear on the ice-field, with no mother bear to look after it.

"Oh, what a little darling!" said Gud, clasping the creature tenderly in her arms.

But then a difficulty arose. The baby bear required milk, and milk was one of the things the tribe never possessed, for they were hunters who pursued animals and killed them for food. Rindar gave the bear some meat, but this only made the poor little creature unwell.

Then the chief came to the conclusion that the kindest thing would be to leave the bear behind.

"Its mother will find it and look after it," he said.

"No; the poor thing will die of hunger," said Gud, beginning to cry at the thought of it. " Dwarfie said its mother must have fallen down a crevice in the ice and got killed. Do find some milk, Daddie ! "

Rindar wanted to please his daughter, for she was the delight of his life. He sat and thought for a while by the fire at the mouth of the cave, and then put on his thickest clothes and went out. But, instead of taking his spear with him, he took some of the ropes the women made by cutting the hides of animals into strips.

crept up to them, and at last got so close that he was able to thrown his leather rope over the fawn's head. Then, very slowly and gently, he began to draw the fawn away, and the mother reindeer followed.

It took him some time, crawling on his hands and knees with the rope tied around his own body, to get the fawn away from the herd. Naturally, the little animal began to struggle for its mother, and the mother tried to find out what was the

RINDAR GOT ON HIS FEET AND LED THE FAWN, AND THE MOTHER REINDEER FOLLOWED

Two miles away he caught sight of a herd of reindeer, and, dropping down on hands and knees, began to creep toward them. As he had taken care to approach from the side opposite to that from which the wind was blowing the big deer with their branching horns were not able to scent him ; and as there were patches of snow upon the ground and he was covered with white furs the reindeer never noticed him as he drew near to them.

The herd was widely scattered, and at some distance from the main body a mother reindeer was feeding with her fawn. Rindar

matter. She smelled suspiciously at the leather rope, but was afraid to leave the fawn and go to the strange white thing crawling along the ground in front.

Still moving very gently, Rindar got on his feet when nearing the caves, and led the fawn into the camp. The mother reindeer followed, and, by tying the fawn to a post in a small unoccupied cave and letting the mother reindeer come in, both animals were at last secured.

It was all very skilfully done, but the hardest part of the task still remained. It was the Dwarf who now stepped in and offered to milk the mother reindeer. He allowed her first to feed her fawn, and brought some grass for her to eat, and then he tried to milk her. She kicked and reared and plunged, but after some minutes the Dwarf came out with quite a nice lot of milk for the baby bear. To the great joy of its little mistress, the bear drank the milk greedily, and then went to sleep huddled up in her arms.

Rindar at first watched this with a smile: but he soon grew thoughtful, and at night he called his men around him and held a council.

"What we have done for the little bear," he said, "we must do for the tribe. How often we have to go hungry because we can get no meat! How many moons is it since we lost the herd we were following and were nearly starved to death?"

"Thirty moons!" said a young hunter fiercely. "Not a bit did any of us have to eat for six days, and my little girl, whom I loved dearly, died through want of food."

"But if we kept a herd of reindeer," said the chief, "there would be milk for our little ones and flesh for us all to eat. We have tamed one deer. Why can we not tame more, and breed from them?"

There was a shout of joy from the men as Rindar revealed his wonderful plan.

Then the hunters gripped their spears, for a woman's shriek rang wildly out in the darkness.

A huge white form flashed by, dimly seen in the light of the camp fire. The baby bear tumbled from the little girl's sleepy arms and crawled away. The great white thing picked up the little bear with its teeth, and then vanished into the night.

"The mother bear!" cried the Dwarf. "She came for her young. I thought she was dead. What a scent she must have! Well, but we shan't want any milk now."

"We want it more than ever," said Rindar. "Every man get a good long rope and follow me."

The chief led his men out to the plain where he had captured the fawn, and the next morning they brought a small herd of reindeer back to the camp.

Man had begun his work of taming animals and keeping them for his use instead of hunting them down to slay them.

HOW MARGARET WILSON GAVE UP HER LIFE

THE name of Margaret Wilson will never be forgotten in Scotland. She was the daughter of a Scottish farmer who lived about 250 years ago. There was a great persecution going on in Scotland, and all people who would not worship God in the way the law ordered were put in prison, and often killed.

Margaret Wilson was put in prison, though quite a young girl, with an older woman, Margaret McLauchlan. Soon afterward she was sentenced to death, but her father went to Edinburgh and persuaded the council to pardon her. The pardon, however, had to be sent to London to be signed, and the council never intended that she should really be reprieved, for before the pardon could come back from London they ordered the two women to be put to death.

So on May 11, 1685, the two Margarets were tied to two stakes driven into the bed of the river at low tide. The stake to which Margaret Wilson was fastened was higher up the bank than the other, and just behind it, so that she could see all that happened to her companion. A large crowd of people stood by waiting to see the end.

Slowly the tide came in, and soon the older woman was drowning. The last sounds she heard in life were the strains of the twenty-fifth Psalm sung by her companion higher up the bank. The soldiers thought Margaret Wilson would give up her religion when she saw that her friend was dead, but they were wrong. Calmly, as the water rose about her, she opened her Bible and read aloud the eighth chapter of Romans: "Who shall separate us from the love of Christ?" Then she bent her head and prayed, and while her eyes were closed the water crept up and swept over her.

"Give her one last chance!" shouted the people. So they drew her up and asked her this question:

"Will you obey the law, and worship God as the law orders?"

"No," was her reply, "I cannot. I am one of Christ's children. Let me go."

So they let her down again and abandoned her to her fate.

When it was all over, and the tide had gone back, their friends cut the cords that bound the two Margarets and carried away the bodies. They buried them together in the quiet graveyard at Wigtown.